TO BURY
—OR—
TO BURN

REVEREND DR. LUKE MITCHELL, JR.

Order this book online at www.trafford.com
or email orders@trafford.com

Most Trafford titles are also available at major online book retailers.

Printed in the United States of America.

ISBN: 978-1-4669-5942-2 (sc)
ISBN: 978-1-4669-5944-6 (hc)
ISBN: 978-1-4669-5943-9 (e)

Library of Congress Control Number: 2012917340

Trafford rev. 09/10/2014

 www.trafford.com

North America & international
toll-free: 1 888 232 4444 (USA & Canada)
fax: 812 355 4082

CONTENTS

INTRODUCTION

In my opinion, one of our greatest struggles as a people has been identifying who we are. We, as a people of color, have allowed other ethnic groups to identify who we are, which has caused a great deal of pain and suffering in America. Our race has an "identity crisis" that has evolved into being identified by many names. These names include Negro, nigger, colored, black, just to name a few, and in recent times included the name "African American."

America, being what it is—a melting pot of cultures and traditions, has made us as a people look at, analyze, and address our various traditions and cultural challenges that are seen through the eyes of people of other ethnic cultures. The printed and broadcast media is often the medium in which we, as a people, are seen and judged by the world. Oftentimes, what others see is not necessarily who we are.

As a people of color, none of the names of the past have associated us to a people, a tradition, a land, or a custom. Therefore, the most recent identification of African American is one that I wholeheartedly embrace because like other cultures it identifies us to a land. Like Asian Americans, Italian Americans, Native Americans, and German Americans, the designation as an African American identifies us with a land, customs, and traditions.

The society at large dictates its culture from traditions handed down by the ancestors of that particular ethnic group. Whether there be Asians, Germans, Italians, Mexicans, etc., most have developed their cultures and traditions from the land of their ancestry. Upon arriving in America, whether voluntary or involuntary, with a ticket or in the hull of a ship, those traditions follow them into this "land of the free and the home of the brave"—this melting pot of cultures called America.

When children of other ethnic and cultural backgrounds are born in America, they don't lose their culture or traditions; they Americanize them in some instances and expand them in others, but the basic foundational tenants of their tradition remain.

This writing is from my personal experience of growing up in a Christian family with deep Southern roots and African heritage. My parents were born and reared in Edgefield and Johnson, South Carolina, where I spent many a summer looking at the cotton fields and listening to stories and laughter of how my father and mother courted in between picking cotton and peaches. Their church activities and burial societies in this rural community had also been a topic of family discussions. The visits to the family burial grounds had always been of interest to me as I viewed the dates of birth and death on the grave markers of my ancestors.

We did not possess a lot of material wealth, but we were rooted in the richness of an African heritage in America with God, family, and community.

The views and opinions that I will try to express are personal as well as professional starting from my vivid childhood memories and experiences as a young boy who visited this small cotton growing community in South Carolina and regularly experienced the country church and the country church burial ground to my present experiences as the pastor of an African American church community in Washington, DC, with deep roots in the south.

I have experienced the dying of my elders and other family members and participated in the planning, the preparation, and the preaching of many funerals throughout my ministerial career of twenty-one years. I have stood at the graveside and said "ashes to ashes and dust to dust" and have watched the remains being slowly lowered beneath the ground. But now some "new players" have entered the stage in this drama called death, and their roles have significantly changed some of our traditions and cultures—"Cremation." Now, as a professional minister, I am faced with African American Christian and non-Christian families who must struggle with the decision of an untraditional disposition of the remains of their loved one.

When I came to New Mount Olive in 1987, I was besieged in my first few months with the deaths of many of the older members, whom we called "seasoned citizens" who had united with the church under my predecessor of forty-four years.

Dr. William Weaver, who was the third pastor of the New Mount Olive Baptist Church, was called from labor to reward in 1985 at the age of eighty-six. Those of his generation and his pastorate also began to follow him in death. There were times when I had two and sometimes three funerals in one week, and I had the urgent need to develop a system to address this critical time in my pastoral ministry.

I organized the condolence ministry whose duties were to help bereaving families through their time of death and preparation. Those individuals were trained in bereavement care and service. Through time, this ministry has developed into one of the greatest tools of my pastorate. The coordinator of this ministry meets with the family at the church in a professional and caring atmosphere. The coordinator prays with the family and through questions and answers assesses the family's emotional stability and financial ability to carry out the task that lies ahead in a productive manner. We, as a church family, have an obligation to care for our membership and their immediate family at death. Therefore, our homegoing services are usually restricted to members in "good standing" and their immediate family, not just the immediate family members, but relatives and friends of the deceased.

Old beliefs and customs are remembered and acted upon. An old belief is that the dead cannot be buried on a rainy day. The sun is a sign that the heavens are open and welcoming of the deceased one. If it rains while a man is dying or if lightning strikes near his house, it is believed the devil has come for the soul. Thus, the family members often attempt to bury the dead on a sunny day.

There is usually a three—to five-day period of preparation before the actual funeral. Before the funeral takes place, there is generally a ceremony known as the wake. At this time, close friends of the family of the deceased pay respects to the family and view the body. Many wakes take place at the funeral parlor, but many have been known to take place at the church or the home of the deceased. This is a time when everyone gathers and eats food cooked by the family members and shares memories of the deceased.

Many of the traditions of the African American Church Community may not be practiced by every African American Independent Church, for independency lends itself to diversity.

In the context of ministry, I have changed the ideology from funeral rituals at New Mount Olive Baptist Church to an idea of celebrating the life, love, and legacy of an individual through a process called "The Homegoing Service."

One of my cornerstone statements at New Mount Olive for a funeral is: "funerals are held at funeral homes. We are gathered here today in the church of the Living God to celebrate the life of our brother or sister . . . this is a homegoing service.``

People who favor cremation tend to be critical of the funeral industry and have advocated funeral reform. In order to determine whether the growing impetus toward funeral reform was that of a vocal minority or reflectively of a broader attitudinal shift among Americans, a survey done in 1965 showed interviews of two groups; one composed of memorial society members and the other of the general public. Memorial society members, who were the primary initiators of funeral reform, tended to advocate cremation and body donation, preplanning final arrangements, and reducing funeral costs.

This group is the most anxious to avoid or disguise death, as indicated by their desire to eliminate the body from the funeral, their greater avoidance of funerals, and their greater reluctance to permit their children to attend a funeral. It appears that, though memorial society members may have been leading the funeral reform efforts in 1965, dissatisfaction with funerals extended beyond this group into the general public. Slightly less than half of the general public was pleased with the present-day funerals and about one-third of them agreed with the memorial group's criticisms. The criticisms suggested that funerals should be simpler, less formal, and more personalized and should impose less of a financial and emotional burden on those attending. The majority of the general public believed that the funeral still met the emotional needs of the bereaved, while the majority of the memorial group believed it did not. About 30 percent of each group indicated that the purpose of funerals is to pay the last respects to the deceased, while about 20 percent of each group indicated that the funeral was for the bereaved to be comforted by others.

CHAPTER 1

THE PRACTICE—
THE HOMEGOING SERVICE

The traditional term "funeral" has always been associated with grief and pain for the most part. The funeral rituals in many cases are not times of healing but more of prolonged hurt. Traditionally, the funeral has not only been a time but a place of mourning also. It's a place that tends to constantly reinforce the reality of death for both the young and old.

Death has always been taboo—a forbidden topic of discussion. However, in the African American community, death is very much an important aspect of culture. It has been stated that death traditions, customs, procedures, mourning practices, burial rites, and even the structure of African American cemeteries differ greatly from that of non-African Americans.

It has been stated amongst the African American community that death is not a time of sadness but a time to celebrate, for the deceased does not have to endure the trials and tribulations of this world. The deceased are indeed mourned and missed; however, death is also a time of celebration.

Many African Americans may not be aware that some of the present-day traditions and customs of death can be traced back to African roots of the Bakongo and the LaDogaa tribes.

These African traditions have been handed down through generations from the oldest living members of the community, in the form of expressions, sayings, superstitions, religious beliefs and practices, and music. Many of the stories relating to death and burials are still believed today.

Death to African Americans is not an event which just occurs, is "handled," and then forgotten about. When one dies, there are a series of events that usually take place. After the approach of death, family members are often notified right away.

The days that lie ahead are challenging days for the deceased's immediate family, church family, community, and pastor. All must work together to achieve a meaningful and effective homegoing celebration. The following is a partial list of our preparation efforts:

1. The immediate family usually contacts the church office.
2. The pastor would either make a pastoral call or visit.
3. The family usually agrees on a date and time to come to the church office to begin the process of planning the service.
4. In that meeting, the family and the coordinator of the condolence ministry will discuss the details of the service which includes, but is not limited to, the preparation of the deceased, the obituary, the program, the repast, and the burial site of the body, whether burial would be local or the body transported for burial in another jurisdiction.

5. The condolence ministry not only does pre-service facilitation, but they are also responsible, along with the administrative staff, for aftercare; the follow-up process encourages the family to *show up for life*.

CHAPTER 2

THE PREPARATION—
THE HOMEGOING SERVICE

Homegoing Celebration Questionnaire

1. How has Pastor Mitchell's approach to funerals differed from other?

   a. Other churches
   b. At New Mount Olive

2. Do you know the difference between a funeral service and a homegoing celebration?
3. How has your experience in funeral services differed from your experience at New Mount Olive?
4. Did you leave New Mount Olive feeling different from what you did when you first came in from this experience?
5. What was the most lasting word, scripture, phrase, or person that impacted your life?

CHAPTER 3

THE PARTICIPATION— THE HOMEGOING SERVICE

The "homegoing service" at New Mount Olive is a family affair, including the church, family, and friends. The immediate family, friends, and church family all come together for the sole purpose of celebrating the life, love, and legacy of the deceased. We still maintain some traditional values such as the wake the night before the homegoing service. Many of our older members and their families prefer this model rather than the more modern wake and homegoing on the same day. Instead of using the traditional terminology of "wake," we use the expression "the family hour," where family and friends fellowship and view the remains in an informal and celebratory atmosphere. Then, at a prearranged time, the formal celebration begins.

CHAPTER 4

THE NEW PARADIGM—
CREMATION

When I came to New Mount Olive in 1987, fifteen years ago, one of my greatest ministerial challenges was to counsel one of the leading families of the church where I was the pastor. The deceased was an adult male who was not a member of the church but the son of a member in good standing. The procedures and responsibilities of how we, as a church family, would respond to members who experience death in their family had already been discussed, agreed on, and made a part of church records. I was faced with a ministerial crisis that I had never experienced. The family was in need of financial assistance to help in the funeral arrangements for their loved one. A request was made from the mother for thousands of dollars to help with the burial expenses of her son. We, as a church, were not financially able to lend that type of assistance. And whatever decision I would make would set precedence for funerals in the future. With regret, the request was denied, but the disposing of the body was still at hand. With much prayer and meditation, I began to seek out information on cremation from my peers and acquaintances, including my father, who served as a pastor of a traditional Baptist congregation and ministered for over thirty years. There was no help to be found from my peers, African American preachers, on the subject of cremation or a service of any type for cremains. The only solution that I could give to a grieving mother was cremation for her son. She freaked out! The question for the immediate family, church family, and the pastor was "How will we bring the decision of disposition to a close?"

The subject of cremation had to be addressed for the disposing of the body. After consultation with the mother and siblings, I convinced them that cremation is an "accelerated process of the inevitable." If accepted, the cost of burial would be greatly reduced from thousands of dollars to hundreds of dollars for cremation. The next challenge was to put together a dignified, yet meaningful service.

CHAPTER 5

THE PAST—CREMATION

The origin of cremation, I have concluded, is unknown. But European archaeologists have tried to place some significant historical events where individuals of secular history and religious history were cremated.

The word cremation comes from the Latin word *cremo* which means "to burn"—particularly the burning of the dead. Cremation generally involves the application of high temperature, typically between fourteen hundred and twenty-one hundred degrees Fahrenheit, to a wooden box or casket which contains a dead body. The body and container are almost completely consumed; the cremated remains consist of bone fragments and particles, which weigh from four to eight pounds. They are then finely ground into granule form. The entire process takes three to five hours. The remains are removed and placed in a container, usually wooden, porcelain, or cardboard, provided by the crematory or the family.

The American way of cremation has greatly evolved from some historical records. Ancient cremation can be traced during biblical times, such as Genesis 38:24, Leviticus 20:14, Leviticus 21:9, Joshua 7:15-25, and 1 Samuel 31:11-13, just to name a few.

From my professional ministerial observation and statistical data from sources such as the Funeral & Memorial Information Council, the Cremation Association of North America, the African American Funeral Industry, and others, the disposition of the deceased by cremation in the African American community has greatly increased over the past fifteen years.

On December 6, 1876, in the small town of Washington, Pennsylvania, the corpse of Baron Joseph Henry Louis Charles De Palm went up in flames in an event billed as the first cremation in modern America. Supporters hailed the event, the first cremation in modern America, as a harbinger of a new age of scientific progress and ritual simplicity. Opponents denounced it as Satan's errand. Reporters too were divided. Some wrote up the story as a tragedy, others as a comedy. Either way, the event was a grand triumph for the US cremation movement.

Between 1876 and 1884, only twenty-eight formally recorded cremations occurred in the United States like in England; some American physicians advocated cremation as a remedy to public health problems. Some Protestant clergy, primarily in New England and the Great Lakes region, and German Freethinkers in California also advocated cremation. Interested in burial reform, they promoted cremation as a humanitarian act. State cremation societies were organized to change the public prejudice against cremation, which is still often viewed as cruel and as a quick, cheap, easy, ceremony less way to solve an uninvited problem. At the same time, however, undertakers advanced their own reforms. With the need to transport corpses to homes from the Civil War and the growing geographic dispersion of the American population, they introduced new embalming practices and cosmetic restoration into the traditional funeral. In 1913, the Cremation Society of America was formed (now known as the Cremation Association of North America (CANA)), but contrary to the membership and goals of the state organizations, its members were not funeral reformers promoting cremation but funeral industry professionals advocating memorialization. These practices, combined with state and national lobbying efforts, deepened the funeral industry's influence on American funerals.

The 1960s and 1970s were a period of tremendous social instability in the United States. The opening of universities to the public resulted in a dramatic increase in college-educated citizens whose education provided them with a secular framework from which to view the world. Social and geographic mobility distanced family members and loosened the grip of family and community tradition. These changes allowed, or required, people to reevaluate the most fundamental cultural values. Ideologies and institutions were scrutinized and were often found lacking. Taboos such as sex and death could not remain hidden. Mainstream religious affiliation declined sharply, especially among Liberal Protestant denominations, which tend to allow individualistic religious views and which have been closely aligned with American culture. The philosophy of secular humanism became popular, as was the continuing influence of existentialism. People experimented with altered states of mind through drug use as well as with alternative forms of healing. The environmental movement expressed holism and concern for the natural world. Social movements demanded civil rights for ethnic minorities, and the consumer movement pushed for individuals to get a fair share from businesses. The threat of atomic annihilation, made clear during World War II, hovered in the background while American citizens experienced extensive, televised coverage of the Vietnam War. In such a volatile time, when individuals and society were threatened, ritual, which is intended to calm and reintegrate, had no such effort on a large segment of society. Ritual too was being scrutinized and was often found inadequate, pretentious, or empty. It was during this period that US cremation rates began to rise.

CHAPTER 6

THE PRESENT—WHO CHOOSES CREMATION

Highly educated individuals tend to be more likely, than those with less education, to choose cremation, as are individuals with high incomes, those in professional occupations, and the upwardly and geographically mobile.

In terms of religion, individuals who choose cremation tend to be antireligious, non-affiliates, members of non-traditional religions, or Protestants. When religiously affiliated, they are less active in their religion than those who choose earth burial.

In terms of US region of residence, people who live in the Pacific and New England states may tend to choose cremation rather than earth burial since agitation for funeral reform and advocacy of cremation have been prevalent in these two regions as have high levels of religious non-affiliation.

A study of cremation in England, the nation with which the United States has the closest cultural ties, states that individuals who choose cremation are urban, suburban, or newly rural residents whereas those who choose earth burial tend to be long-term rural dwellers. American studies have not addressed rural and urban differences in the method of body disposition, but studies suggest that this may be relevant.

Age does not differentiate individuals by the method of body disposition. However, religious participation is higher among the elderly than among other groups, and the elderly are more likely than other age groups to consider their religious background the most important factor influencing their attitudes toward death.

One characteristic of those who advocate cremation is lower familiarity with funeral ritual as evidenced by those having attended fewer funerals than those who choose earth burial. An additional characteristic is that cremationists tend to make monetary donations to secular charities in lieu of sending flowers to a funeral whereas people who choose burial tend to send flowers and, if making monetary donations, donate to religious organizations.

A 1990 study of cremation in England found that people are slightly more likely to choose burial for a loved one than for themselves. The study suggests that people are unconcerned about their own identity and status after death but want to remember deceased loved ones. Since people are generally aware of the possibility of combining memorialization with cremation, they associate burial with remembrance and cremation with forgetfulness. The experience with funerals impacted the chosen method of body disposition among students. Those who had never been to a funeral chose cremation for themselves, but after attending a cremation and a burial, they switched their preference to burial. In considering this change in opinion, the study noted the contradiction between students' perception and concern that cremation is clinical and impersonal compared with the naturalness of burial; yet they expressed preference for the rapid destruction of the body rather than its slow decay. With burial, the body decomposes slowly in nature's time. With cremation, decomposition is rapid and corresponds to clock time.

People who favor cremation tend to be critical of the funeral industry and advocate funeral reform. In order to determine whether the growing impetus toward funeral reform was that of a vocal minority or reflectively of a broader attitudinal shift among Americans, a survey done in 1965 showed interviews of two groups: one composed of memorial society members and the other of the general public. Memorial society members, who were the primary initiators of funeral reform, tended to advocate cremation and body donation, preplanning final arrangements, and reducing funeral costs.

CHAPTER 7

THE PURPOSE— CREMATION

I have counseled with many families since 1987, who have experienced the decision of disposition, and have asked them how did they come to the decision of cremation over traditional burial rites. Over the years, I have been pleasantly surprised about their rationale, from the cremation of the young to my most recent, the cremation of one of the admired mothers of our church. Some of the reasons ranged from economics to the freedom for untraditional memorialization. One stunning example of a mother's request for cremation was that her children would not have to come and be attached and committed to a "place" on earth for the rest of their lives. They could live with the memory of a mother who set them free from that type of continued pain and obligation.

CHAPTER 8

THE PLANNING—
CREMATION

Because we are a people who are deeply rooted in some form of religious and ritual activity, the reality of death finds us, from time to time, pondering over our very own mortality. For the African American Christian, our God consciousness plays a part in the everyday activities of our lives and is not decreased or minimized upon our death. Therefore, if one chooses cremation over traditional burial rites the need to not dechristianize this new paradigm must be addressed. The caregiver or the minister should have a healthy understanding and respect of the need for cremation and not stand as an advocate of cremation being a dechristianization, or lessening of values, of an individual's last rite of dignity in death. Since cremation is a new paradigm of the disposing of remains for the African American community, the minister does not have to be locked in by tradition in carrying out the service in a dignified and effective manner. He must be flexible and open to creativity during the planning of a memorialization of the deceased.

There are many ways to carry out an effective memorial service if the minister is open-minded and open-hearted enough to step beyond the comforts of tradition and walk beyond the pulpit and the pews to accomplish a means to an end. If he finds himself in a position that the church's posture is not healthy toward cremation, he need not shove it down their throats, but begin a strategic process in raising the consciousness of his congregation toward this new paradigm by using Bible study, seminars, workshops, private discussions, and representatives of the funeral industry.

CHAPTER 9

THE POSSIBILITIES— CREMATION

If the minister can raise his consciousness to embrace choice, he will also raise the consciousness of his congregation and others whom he may have the opportunity to serve. In that process, the possibility of being a church of even more inclusiveness can be achieved.

The embracing of cremation or even the understanding of its value in the African American community can be used as another evangelistic tool that could possibly bring people into an atmosphere of untraditional practices and values. Christ can be introduced in a traditional environment as well as an untraditional environment, in the church or outside of her sacred walls, in the funeral home facilities, or even as one helping the family to scatter the ashes of their loved one from the side of a boat or the top of a mountain. You will undeniably create a special place in the hearts and minds of the family and friends of those who have shared in the process.

Death has no respect for person; therefore, the minister should have no respect for the person to whom he renders his ministerial services. We are in an age where the Words of Jesus are true: "I have sheep that are not of this fold," and because individuals that we must minister to may not all talk like us, look like us, live like us, or even hold our traditional values, it does not mean that they are not sheep that are in need of a shepherd. Because many of our traditional church values have come under attack in recent years, we should as professionals look through the challenge and ask ourselves the question, why? The church is still evolving and still being made the Bride of Christ, and with that evolution, we must begin to understand, if not embrace, the issues of this day and time. Cremation is only one of many issues that beg our attention and voice in the African American Independent Church community.

TEST AND ANALYSIS

This project is being tested through

- interviews with African American families and individuals who have been confronted with the decision of untraditional disposition
- questionnaires.

The analysis of the project will be from

- commissioned reports,
- statistics from leaders in the funeral industry.

GLOSSARY

African American—of or relating to Americans of African ancestry.

Afrocentricity—African-centered.

Burial Ground—location of burying a corpse.

Casket—a coffin.

Ceremony—a formal act or set of acts performed as prescribed by ritual or custom.

Comminglings—to blend or cause to blend together.

Context—the part of a written or spoken statement that surrounds a word or passage and that often specifies its meaning.

Controversy—a dispute characterized by the expression of opposing views.

Corpse—a dead body, especially the body of a deceased human being.

Cremains—ashes remaining after the cremation of a corpse.

Cremation—to incinerate.

Crematory—a furnace or establishment for the cremation of corpses.

Culture—the totality of socially transmitted behavior patterns, arts, beliefs, institutions, and all other products of human work and thought typical of a population or community at a given time.

Customs—a practice followed as a matter of course among a people.

Dechristianization—lessening of values.

Dechristianize—dismissal of the worth of values.

Dignity—the quality or condition of being esteemed, honored, or worthy.

Disposal—a particular method of dealing with or settling matters.

Disposition—a final settlement.

Evangelistic—Tool—a method used in proclaiming the Gospel.

Funeral Industry—a branch of manufacture dealing with the ceremonies held in connection with the burial or cremation of the dead.

Inclusiveness—taking much or everything within its scope.

Melting Pot—a place where immigrants of different races or cultures form an integrated society.

Memorialization—to present a memorial to.

Memorialize—to commemorate.

Methodology—the system of principles, procedures, and practices applied to a particular branch of knowledge.

Paradigm—a list of all the inflectional forms of a word taken as an example of the conjugation to which it belongs.

Personalization—to personify.

Pre-arrangement—to make prior plans or preparations.

Ritual—the prescribed form or order of conducting a religious or solemn ceremony.

Sociological—the study of human social behavior.

Taboo—a prohibition excluding something from use, approach or mention because of its sacred and inviolable nature

Tenants —an occupant, inhabitant, or dweller in a place.

Tradition—transmittal of elements of a culture from one generation to another.

Traditional—customs and usages transmitted from one generation to another and viewed as a coherent body of precedents influencing the present.

BIBLIOGRAPHY

Unless otherwise noted, Scripture quotations are from the King James Version of the Bible.

Scripture quotations marked (AKJV) are from the Amplified King James Version of the Bible.

Baker, B. S. *Special Occasions in the Black Church*. Nashville, TN: Broadman Press, 1989.

Bugen, L. A. *Death and Dying: Theory, Research and Practice*. Dubuque, IA: William C. Brown Company, 1979.

Carney, Karen L. *Our Special Garden: Understanding Cremation*. Wethersfield, CT: N. P., 1995.

Cremation Association of North America, 1913 *History of Cremation*.

Doka, K. J. *Living With Grief After Sudden Loss, Suicide, Homicide, Accident, Heart Attach, Stroke*, Washington, DC: Hospice Foundation of America, 1996.

Encyclopedic Britannica@Britannica.com, *Burial*.

Encyclopedic Britiannica@Britannica.com, *Funeral Customs*.

Platt, L. A. *Death and Dying, Volume I: Grief and Bereavement: A Research Biography, 1964-1984.* Georgia Southern College: The Social Gerontology Program, 1985.

Platt, L. A., Branch, R. G., Perisco, R. and Hill, D. E. (eds.) *Encounters with Death, Dying and Bereavement.* Lexington, MA: Ginn Press, 1986.

Platt, L. A. and Branch, R. G. *Resources for Ministry in Death and Dying.* Nashville, TN: Broadman Press, 1988.

Protero, S. R. *Purified By Fire, A History of Cremation in America.* Berkeley and Los Angeles, CA: University of California Press, 2001.

Shriver, G. H. and Leonard, B. J. *Encyclopedia of Religious Controversies in the United States.* Westport, CT: Greenwood Press, 1997.

Wirthlin Worldwide. *Study of American Attitudes Toward Ritualization and Memorialization. Executive Summary of the Funeral and Memorial Information Counsel.* 1999, Updated 2000.

NOTES

www.ingramcontent.com/pod-product-compliance
Lightning Source LLC
Chambersburg PA
CBHW061229280526
45784CB00006B/2697